"The proble[m of evil arises] in every gen[eration ...] ful book is a superb resource for thinking deeply about it and responding with compassion and clarity."
Andrew Wilson, Teaching Pastor, King's Church London

"This is a very helpful book for those who wrestle with the presence of evil in our world. I consider myself one of those strugglers. This book encouraged me to keep wrestling with an eye to the much bigger picture of all that God has done, is doing, and will do."
Randy Newman, Late Senior Fellow for Apologetics and Evangelism, C. S. Lewis Institute; author, *Questioning Faith* and *Bringing the Gospel Home*

"As a counselor, I have seen the desperate urgency of hurting people asking how God could allow their pain. At the heart of this concise, tender, humble, and intellectually honest book is the best answer we can possibly give: 'God is not asking for silence . . . [or] demanding the stiff upper lip.' Instead, he welcomes our cry for justice as the echo of his own. Thoughtful and highly contextualized for our current cultural instincts, Hansen's book is easy to recommend."
J. Alasdair Groves, Executive Director, Christian Counseling & Educational Foundation; coauthor, *Untangling Emotions*

"The problem of evil, and in particular the Holocaust, is the greatest challenge to faith. From a biblical and pastoral perspective, Hansen tackles this challenge with boldness and compassion. While not offering easy answers, he argues how the Christian faith offers hope and justice amid the greatest evil imaginable."

    Sean McDowell, Associate Professor of Christian Apologetics, Biola University; author, *A New Kind of Apologist*

"What I love about this book is that Hansen grapples with evil and suffering not as a notional or abstract concept but by forcing the reader to reckon with some of the twentieth century's most agonizing moral events, particularly Hitler's and Stalin's brutality. Hansen ably communicates how the Christian worldview—chiefly, Jesus himself—helps explain our agonies and ultimately remedies them. What an irony it is that one of Christianity's chief objections—the problem of suffering—can become one of its greatest testimonies."

    Andrew T. Walker, Associate Professor of Christian Ethics and Public Theology, The Southern Baptist Theological Seminary; Fellow, The Ethics and Public Policy Center

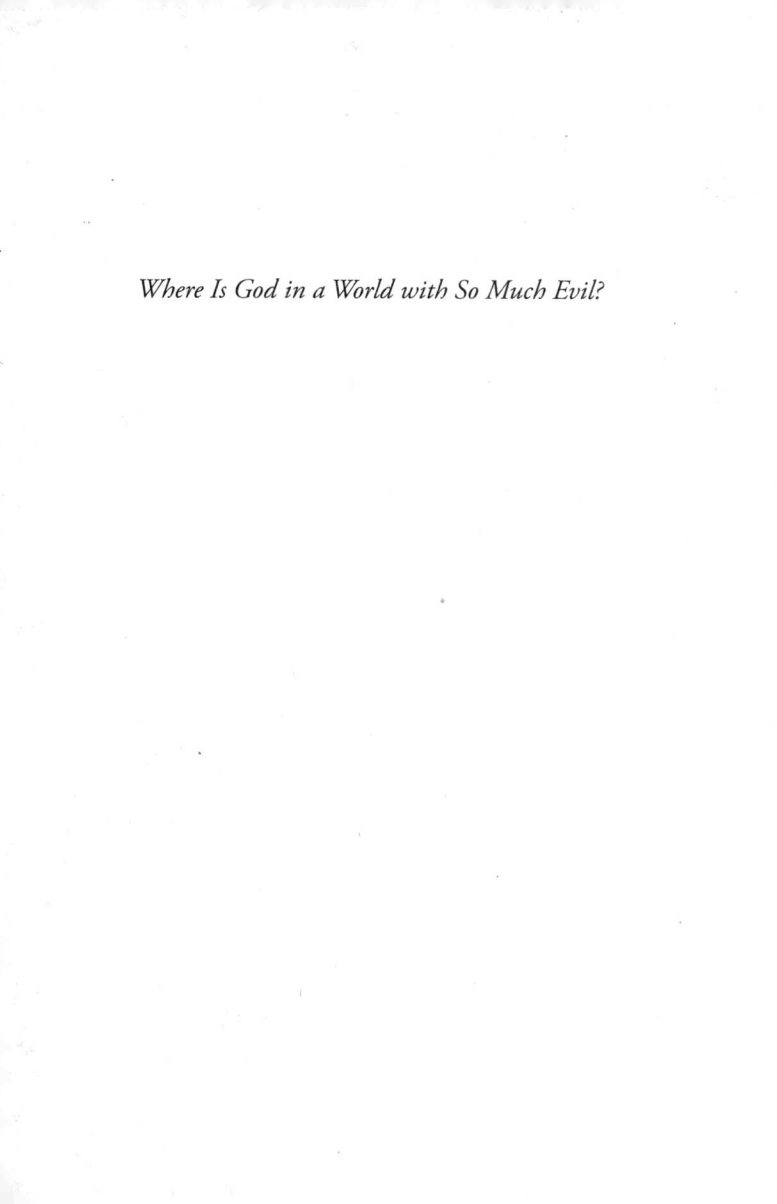

Where Is God in a World with So Much Evil?

TGC Hard Questions

Jared Kennedy, Series Editor

Did the Resurrection Really Happen?, Timothy Paul Jones
Does God Care about Gender Identity?, Samuel D. Ferguson
Is Christianity Good for the World?, Sharon James
What Does Depression Mean for My Faith?, Kathryn Butler, MD
Where Is God in a World with So Much Evil?, Collin Hansen
Why Do We Feel Lonely at Church?, Jeremy Linneman

Where Is God in a World with So Much Evil?

Collin Hansen

:: CROSSWAY®

WHEATON, ILLINOIS

Where Is God in a World with So Much Evil?

© 2025 by Collin Hansen

Published by Crossway
        1300 Crescent Street
        Wheaton, Illinois 60187

All rights reserved. No part of this publication may be reproduced, stored in a retrieval system, or transmitted in any form by any means, electronic, mechanical, photocopy, recording, or otherwise, without the prior permission of the publisher, except as provided for by USA copyright law. Crossway® is a registered trademark in the United States of America.

Cover design: Ben Stafford

Cover image: Unsplash

First printing 2025

Printed in the United States of America

Scripture quotations are from the ESV® Bible (The Holy Bible, English Standard Version®), © 2001 by Crossway, a publishing ministry of Good News Publishers. Used by permission. All rights reserved. The ESV text may not be quoted in any publication made available to the public by a Creative Commons license. The ESV may not be translated in whole or in part into any other language.

Trade paperback ISBN: 978-1-4335-9800-5
ePub ISBN: 978-1-4335-9802-9
PDF ISBN: 978-1-4335-9801-2

Library of Congress Cataloging-in-Publication Data

Names: Hansen, Collin, 1981– author
Title: Where is God in a world with so much evil? / Collin Hansen.
Description: Wheaton, Illinois : Crossway, 2025. | Series: TGC hard questions | Includes bibliographical references and index.
Identifiers: LCCN 2024005904 (print) | LCCN 2024005905 (ebook) | ISBN 9781433598005 trade paperback | ISBN 9781433598029 epub | ISBN 9781433598012 pdf
Subjects: LCSH: Justice—Religious aspects—Christianity
Classification: LCC BS680.J8 H36 2025 (print) | LCC BS680.J8 (ebook) | DDC 261.8—dc23
LC record available at https://lccn.loc.gov/2024005904
LC ebook record available at https://lccn.loc.gov/2024005905

Crossway is a publishing ministry of Good News Publishers.

BP	34	33	32	31	30	29	28	27	26	25
15	14	13	12	11	10	9	8	7	6	5	4	3	2	1

Contents

Where Is God in a World with So Much Evil?   *1*

Notes   *45*

Recommended Resources   *47*

Scripture Index   *49*

WHEN YOU WALK through Yad Vashem, the World Holocaust Remembrance Center in Jerusalem, you're emotionally exhausted by the end. The pain. The suffering. The horror of six million Jews murdered, less than a century ago. Children. Grandmothers. Young. Old. Pregnant. Barren. Gassed and cremated with modern efficiency. In Yad Vashem, you see their faces. You learn their stories. The names. The memories. It breaks your heart.

Shortly before you leave, you see a large photo from the Buchenwald concentration camp. Dated April 16, 1945, it shows inmates sleeping three to a bed, with bunks stacked four high. The bodies are nothing more than skin stretched over skeletons.

Tucked away in the second row of bunks, seventh from the left, is a sixteen-year-old face. I didn't recognize it in the picture, but the face would become famous around the world. It's the face of Elie Wiesel, winner of the Nobel Peace Prize in 1986. His book *Night* recounts his experience of the *Shoah*, or catastrophe.

The Holocaust.

Night is the story of his experience at Auschwitz and why he never slept soundly again. When Wiesel arrived in Auschwitz, he saw babies tossed in a flaming ditch. How was this possible? How could the world be silent when men, women, and children perished in fires? Wiesel heard his father cry for help as SS guards beat him to death. Wiesel didn't move to help him, and he never forgave himself.

He too was silent.

Wiesel wrote:

Never shall I forget that night, the first night in camp,
    which has turned my life into one long night,
    seven times cursed and seven times sealed.
Never shall I forget that smoke.
Never shall I forget the little faces of the children,
    whose bodies I saw turned into wreaths of
    smoke beneath a silent blue sky.
Never shall I forget those flames which consumed
    my faith forever. . . .
Never shall I forget those moments which murdered
    my God and my soul and turned my dreams
    to dust.

Never shall I forget these things, even if I am
> condemned to live as long as God Himself.
Never.[1]

When three Jewish inmates, including a young boy, were hanged at Buchenwald, Wiesel heard a man behind him ask, "Where is merciful God, where is He?"[2]

Silence. The details they witnessed are too gruesome for me to share. The man asked again, "For God's sake, where is God?" A voice answered to Wiesel: "Where He is? This is where—hanging here from this gallows."[3] It was the voice of Wiesel's own conscience. Wiesel became the accuser. God the accused.

Wiesel survived the camps. And so did his belief in God's existence. But his doubt lingered. He could no longer trust God's justice.

How do we account for God's silence amid the greatest of human suffering? Is God dead? Did we kill him? Or do we just put him on trial and find him guilty of crimes against humanity?

Few can relate to the degree of horror Wiesel witnessed and experienced. But probably all of us, Jew and Gentile, have cried out to God in distress and heard nothing in response. Or at least we know and love someone who's felt this way.

If you've worked in ministry, or just tried to share the gospel of Jesus Christ with your friends and family, you've probably heard these skeptical questions: Why doesn't God speak up about evil? Why won't he assure us of his presence in those moments when the universe feels cold, dark, and threatening? This is the hard question I'm trying to help us address in this booklet: Can we trust God when he's silent about evil?

To answer, let us begin by considering why we suffer in the first place.

Moral Revolution—from Jesus to Hitler

Sometimes we assure ourselves that others suffer because they weren't careful or thoughtful. In the early years of the modern state of Israel, many Holocaust survivors carried a stigma. The Jews who spent the 1930s and '40s in the Middle East couldn't understand how six million could have died without more resistance. Surely the victims should have done more, fought back harder. They should have known! "It's not God's fault," some said. "The Jewish leaders were responsible."

The sheer scale of the Holocaust, however, overwhelms any such defense mechanisms. Efforts to fight back—such as the 1943 uprising in the Warsaw ghetto—failed against determined Nazi brutality. There's no way to explain away the scope of this horror by somehow blaming the victims.

When I teach students who are training to lead churches, I ask them to write a sermon that incorporates what they believe is the most powerful objection to Christianity. For me, it's the silence of God in the face of suffering, especially the suffering of children who seem to have done nothing wrong. Sometimes when I'm talking with someone who doesn't share my Christian faith, I'll even ask him or her to consider this question. It's not just that most of us can relate to asking for help and hearing no response. It's that this question of God's silence—especially in the Holocaust—has precipitated nothing less than a moral revolution in Western civilization. Historian Alec Ryrie observes that World War II exposed Christianity as setting the wrong priorities: "It now seemed plain that cruelty, discrimination and murder were evil in a way that fornication, blasphemy and impiety were not."[4]

In other words, the Holocaust transformed our standards for evil. In the shadow of Auschwitz, how could anyone be worried about differences between Christian denominations? Why should anyone care if two adults engage in consensual sex? A little cursing in God's name can't be a big deal when he didn't bother to stop millions of Jews from marching into the gas chambers.

Before the war, Jesus Christ was the most potent moral figure in Western culture. You don't have to look hard for evidence when you travel around Europe today. Just take in the medieval art and visit the ancient churches. In town squares where bells tolled on Sunday mornings, even non-Christians measured themselves according to Jesus's example of love. He set the moral standard in his sinless life.

However, Ryrie argues, the overwhelming tragedy of the war displaced Jesus as the fixed reference point for good and evil.[5] Today the bells still toll, but the pews are usually empty. Art includes Jesus only to be ironic. Across the West today, you can pass nearly every day except Christmas in relative ease and comfort without giving thought to Jesus.

So who replaced Jesus as the new moral standard?

Adolf Hitler.

"It is as monstrous to praise him as it would once have been to disparage Jesus," Ryrie writes. "While Christian imagery, crosses and crucifixes have lost much of their potency in our culture, there is no visceral image which now packs as visceral an emotional punch as a swastika."[6]

If Christians marched down your street behind a cross, you might shrug them off as eccentrics. But if Nazis marched down your street behind a swastika, you would feel their presence as an existential threat to you, your family, and the entire public order. Or consider a street preacher reading Scripture and proclaiming good news of the kingdom of God. He'll probably be ignored. Now consider you're walking the ancient streets of a venerable European city and you see a young man dressed in khaki from head to toe, with a red arm band. He's reading out loud from *Mein Kampf*. He won't last long before violent opposition forms to silence his hateful words.

In this moral revolution, few would pretend to be proud of everything they've said and done. You don't pretend to be perfect. But at least you know this: You wouldn't put up with Hitler. You wouldn't be silent in your protest. Jew and Gentile alike, we know that we need to speak up against such evil because we can't forget the Holocaust.

Problem is, how do you know who's Hitler today without seeing a swastika?

quisitor—Making Ourselves the Standard

ead Wiesel for the first time, his skeptical questions sounded familiar. I knew I'd heard them before—but not about God's silence in the Holocaust. In fact, the accusations had been delivered by an unforgettable character in the nineteenth-century novel *The Brothers Karamazov*, a classic written by renowned Christian author Fyodor Dostoevsky.[7]

In book 5 of the novel, Ivan Karamazov argues with his younger brother, Alyosha, about God. Like Wiesel, Ivan is horrified by the suffering of innocent children. Like Wiesel, Ivan protests against God for allowing injustice. Here's the riveting passage:

> And if the suffering of children goes to make up the sum of suffering needed to buy truth, then I assert beforehand that the whole of truth is not worth such a price. . . . Imagine that you yourself are building the edifice of human destiny with the object of making people happy in the finale, of giving them peace and rest at last, but for that you must inevitably and unavoidably torture just one tiny creature, that same

child who was beating her chest with her little fist, and raise your edifice on the foundation of her unrequited tears—would you agree to be the architect of such conditions?[8]

Dostoevsky calls this chapter "Rebellion." No wonder. Ivan says, "It's not that I don't accept God, Alyosha, I just most respectfully return him the ticket."[9] That's the famous line. Never has a more powerful argument against God been mustered than this: "I believe in him. I just hate him." Turns out there may be something worse than God's silence. It's God trying to offer an explanation we reject as unjust.

In the next chapter, with Ivan's poem "The Grand Inquisitor," Dostoevsky puts Jesus on the literal witness stand. But the trial ends in an unexpected way.

> When the Inquisitor fell silent, he waited some time for his prisoner to reply. His silence weighed on him. He had seen how the captive listened to him all the while intently and calmly, looking him straight in the eye, and apparently not wishing to contradict anything. The old man would have liked him to say something,

even something bitter, terrible. But suddenly he approaches the old man in silence and gently kisses him on his bloodless, ninety-year-old lips. That is the whole answer. The old man shudders.[10]

Silence, and a kiss.

Is that the best Jesus can do? A kiss?

Why won't God speak up and defend himself? Maybe it's because even if he did, we wouldn't listen. No matter what he said, we'd still declare him guilty.

That's why Fyodor Dostoevsky let Ivan put Jesus on trial. He was warning us that when we judge God, we don't replace him with a superior morality. Instead, anything goes. *We* make the rules. But no one's in charge. In Dostoevsky's story, Ivan learns his lesson the hard way. With all of his ranting against God, someone takes Ivan seriously and kills his father. When the killer hands Ivan money stolen from his murdered father, the implications of "anything goes" in a world without God begin to crush Ivan.

Without knowing it, Dostoevsky warned us about how the twentieth century would unfold. It's a fate worse than God's silence. It's a life where we no longer get angry at

God's silence. It's a world where God's voice is a forgotten echo.

It's the Second World War on the Eastern Front.

Where Is Evil Located?

I caught a glimpse of that world through the eyes of another Russian writer, Vasily Grossman, and his epic novel *Life and Fate*. A Jewish journalist in the Soviet Union during World War II, Grossman was one of the first writers to observe a Nazi death camp when Treblinka was liberated in eastern Poland.

I was overcome with emotion when I read one of the novel's scenes where a young child is separated from his parents during the selection for the Treblinka gas chambers. I can hardly write about the story without weeping. A Jewish doctor could have avoided immediate death due to her profession. Instead, she elected to hold the panicked child's hands through the horrifying process, all the way until death. The childless woman had one final thought before she perished: *I've become a mother.*[11]

Life and Fate depicts the evils of Nazism like no other work. I've never seen such a vivid description of the banality of evil in building and operating a gas chamber.

But Grossman didn't depict the Soviets as paragons of virtue just because they weren't Nazis. Despite Grossman's acclaim as a writer and battlefield witness, *Life and Fate* almost didn't survive the Soviet censors. Grossman refused to valorize Stalin for fighting against Hitler. So the Soviets wanted to shut Grossman up, just as they had tried to silence God through state-mandated atheism across Russia and its neighbors.

Grossman, however, retained an objective standard of evil that allowed him to judge both sides. He helped the world to see that communism and fascism weren't so much two ends of a left-right spectrum as mirror images of totalitarian evil. They might have been mortal enemies in ideology and war. But in morality, they were partners in crime. They shared a common goal of silencing God's voice of judgment against their plans for world subjugation.

Grossman died in 1964, nearly a decade before Aleksandr Solzhenitsyn published his *Gulag Archipelago* about the evils of the Soviet state. Solzhenitsyn's shocking account of Soviet prison camps explains why "don't be a Nazi" morality hasn't stopped evil. "I'm not as bad as Hitler" is too low a bar for the justice we expect when someone robs our home or rapes our neighbor. It's too low a bar when innocent children are at stake. We're right to cry out for greater justice.

Anti-Nazi morality also fails because it shifts evil from something *inside* us to something *out there* among our enemies. It leads us to sanctify ourselves and demonize our enemies, moving us from defendant to judge, as if we've become righteous merely by virtue of being born after Hitler's death. Solzhenitsyn, as a Christian, saw evil not just as something "out there" but also "in here." He famously observed, "The line separating good and evil passes not through states, nor between classes, nor between political parties either—but right through every human heart."[12]

I watched the 2022 Beijing Winter Olympics with my children. They delighted in the courageous, gorgeous performances on ice and snow. During the closing ceremonies, my older son asked for a crash course in geopolitics. He saw Russian president Vladimir Putin standing as the honored guest of Chinese president Xi Jinping. I explained that soon many Ukrainian families would be fighting for their lives and homes against invaders from Putin's Russia. Within days Putin launched the largest land war in Europe since the end of World War II.

Aleksandr Solzhenitsyn wouldn't be fooled by Vladimir Putin's pretensions as defender of the Christian faith in our day. Putin justified his invasion of Ukraine—home of Grossman and his mother, who died when the Nazis massacred the Jews of Berdychiv in 1941—as "de-Nazification." The rockets Putin has sent raining down on apartment complexes across Ukraine should remind us: all manner of evil begins when we underestimate the human penchant for self-deception.

We shouldn't miss the point. We need an objective standard of morality bigger than "not Hitler." When we externalize evil to an out-group, we deceive ourselves in self-righteousness. When we don't listen to God, demagogues emerge to speak as if they are gods. Dictators from Hitler to Putin promise easy answers to difficult questions about what's wrong with the world—*The people we already hate are to blame!*—and they promise a godlike ability to enact justice. They build a new kingdom by shedding their enemies' blood.

Maybe the problem isn't the silence of God. Maybe we're just not listening. Or maybe we prefer the sound of our own voices.

A World Where God Isn't Silent

At least in the West, we live with the residue of Christianity. So when skeptics accuse God of silence in the face of evil, they usually still harbor Christian assumptions about good and evil. They want it both ways. They want to judge God. But they want to use a standard of judgment for right and wrong that they learned from God. That's why it feels right to demand a response from God. Because we know he's a God who speaks.

Years ago a friend told me about a man who left his church. This man's experience echoed Job's. He lost children. He lost his marriage. He could no longer bear the suffering. And he blamed God. He wanted nothing to do with church any longer.

Maybe you've counseled someone in this kind of situation. Or maybe you've been in this pit of despair yourself. Surrounded today by secularism, we find it easy to tune out God's voice as an echo from humanity's ignorant past. I think many skeptics like Ivan Karamazov expect peace when they stop raging against a God who isn't there, who is silent. There's some comfort, I suppose, in knowing God isn't just holding out in our misery. We can bear just about anything—except the possibility that God is there but isn't doing anything to help.

But when I think about this man who left his church, I wonder: *What did he gain? Did his suffering end? Did he draw comfort from knowing that his suffering had no purpose, and that no one could come to his aid?*

Imagine a baby finds out her mother isn't nearby. Does the baby stop crying? Would it help to know her mother has left and will never return?

So long as the mother is still in the house, she might eventually hear the cries and bring comfort. Or maybe the mother knows something her baby does not. Maybe Mom knows the baby needs to learn to soothe herself for sleep, and that's why she doesn't rush in to help.

For the person who thinks her problems stem from belief in God, we must gently remind her of the alternatives. When we silence God, we lose whatever purpose he might have ultimately intended. We lose the possibility that justice may be done, if not in this life, then by a God who judges in eternity. We lose the hope that evil will someday end, that goodness will ultimately prevail. And what do we gain? Cold comfort that no one's coming to help, no one will ever hear our cries.

I think we'd rather live in a world where God hears and works in unexpected ways, where he confounds human wisdom. Sometimes comfort comes from being wrong. I talked to a senior US diplomat who visited Ukraine shortly before the invasion in 2022. He begged the Ukrainians to prepare. They didn't. He didn't expect them to last a day. Instead, Russia's initial thrust against Kyiv was repelled. History has a way of catching up with dictators who play God.

When I was growing up, the predominant attitude I picked up from media was *Why can't we just let people do whatever they want (so long as they're not as bad as Hitler)?* Today that attitude sounds naive. The Western conscience has been reawakened. Evil has a name and an address. Ukrainian flags flew nearly everywhere I traveled around the United States and Europe through 2023. We now demand justice.

As I saw this show of support for the oppressed, for Ukrainian children seized and taken into Russian captivity, I realized God isn't silent at all in response to our pleas. Elie Wiesel would have condemned the Russian invaders. He would have denounced Hamas for its 2023 terrorist attacks against civilians, the worst murder of Jews since the Holocaust. Once again we might ask, "Where is God? How can he be silent and allow this evil to repeat?"

But I think God is speaking—loudly. He is not silent at all. We hear his voice in the anguish of Elie Wiesel. We read his words in the complaints of Ivan Karamazov. Even the voices that fault God still testify to his presence. Our very sense of justice tells us that God hears every child's cry. Nazis and Soviets may try to suppress justice by shifting blame toward their enemies. And yet our consciences still cry out. The very expectation that we would hear from God, the very hope for an explanation, reminds us God is at work. Hitler is dead. But we're still reading Wiesel. The Soviet Union has fallen. But we're still learning from Dostoevsky, Solzhenitsyn, and Grossman.

God hears, and speaks, through us. We are the only creatures dignified by his very image. From the beginning, he has been talking to anyone who will listen—or even engage him in debate.

Back before the dawn of creation, there was only silence. Then God spoke in the darkness and there was light (Gen. 1:1–3). And when God finished with night and day, when he finished with the eagles and dolphins and gazelles, he created his greatest masterpiece. On the sixth day of creation, God made man and woman. God created nothing else in his image (Gen. 1:26). Nothing else in his likeness. Only man and woman. What does this mean?

It means the dolphins don't cry out for God in the silence. It means the eagles don't ask, "Where is God?" It means the gazelles don't wonder if they should forgive. Every man, woman, and child—regardless of whether he or she believes in Jesus or acknowledges him as Creator—has been made in his image.

We demand justice because we have been made by a God who is just. We cry out for mercy because we have been made by a God who is merciful. We ask, "Where is God?" when babies burn in the fire, when children walk alone into the gas chamber. God's image can be seen in Elie Wiesel, Vasily Grossman, and everyone else who screams into the dark void. We are the only creatures who argue with God as our Father. Like exasperated teenagers, we shout, "It's not fair!"

And we know something's wrong, because justice doesn't always prevail. We know this is not the world as God made it. But man and woman have rejected God. We, humanity, have gone our own way. We may be made in the image of God, but we deny his parentage. Eve listened to the lies of the serpent over the promises of her Creator. Adam listened to Eve instead of God (Gen. 3:17).

In the aftermath of this catastrophe, it was not God who was silent. Adam and Eve heard God walking in the garden, but they hid from his presence (Gen. 3:8). It was God who spoke. In Genesis 3:9, he asked Adam a simple question: "Where are you?"

We've been asking God the same question ever since.

Now in our exile, east of Eden, evil roars in victory. The human story plays in a minor key. Grief hit home almost immediately when Adam and Eve's righteous son was killed by his jealous brother. There in the garden, the seeds of the Soviet gulag were planted. The lies of the serpent presaged the *Shoah*. Humanity has turned a deaf ear to God and turned in violence on one another.

Job's Night

From Eden, the Hebrew Bible proceeds across the centuries, haunted by questions. Does anyone still listen to God and actually hear him? Who can tell us where to find him amid all this pain and suffering?

Then we meet Job. The book has long been considered among the most important for understanding God's response to innocent suffering. Job was "blameless and upright, one who feared God and turned away from evil" (Job 1:1). We can't blame him for any of the calamities that befall him and his family. They come with God's permission. Despite losing nearly everything but his life, Job still worships God. "Naked I came from my mother's womb, and naked shall I return. The LORD gave, and the LORD has taken away; blessed be the name of the LORD" (Job 1:21).

Job sits destitute in the ashes of the fire that has consumed his servants and sheep, his earthly wealth. He scrapes painful sores with pottery broken in the home that collapsed upon his children (Job 2:8). His wife, shattered with grief, questions her husband and makes a demand: "Do you still hold fast your integrity? Curse God and die" (Job 2:9).

But Job is not like Adam. He will not entertain this tempting. He rebukes his wife: "You speak as one of the foolish women would speak. Shall we receive good from God, and shall we not receive evil?" (Job 2:10).

Job refuses to sin in his speech to God or anyone else. Then his friends show up. They have nothing to say. What could possibly bring Job any comfort? They only raise their voices to weep for a friend they hardly recognize (Job 2:12). For seven days and nights they don't speak a word to Job out of respect for his suffering.

Finally, Job speaks. He erupts in a curse.

How does he lament his lot? How does he describe his destitution?

As night. It's the cold, dark, and threatening night we recognize from Wiesel's concentration camps. Job curses the day he was born, a child innocent to the ways of a cruel world.

> Let the day perish on which I was born,
>   and the night that said,
>   "A man is conceived."
> Let that day be darkness!
>   May God above not seek it,
>   nor light shine upon it.
> Let gloom and deep darkness claim it.
>   Let clouds dwell upon it;
>   let the blackness of the day terrify it.
> That night—let thick darkness seize it!
>   Let it not rejoice among the days of the year;
>   let it not come into the number of the months.

> Behold, let that night be barren;
> let no joyful cry enter it.
> Let those curse it who curse the day,
> who are ready to rouse up Leviathan.
> Let the stars of its dawn be dark;
> let it hope for light, but have none,
> nor see the eyelids of the morning,
> because it did not shut the doors of my mother's womb,
> nor hide trouble from my eyes. (Job 3:3–10)

Now Job's friends can no longer remain silent. Job must somehow be guilty if he's suffered this much (Job 4:7). This too is our temptation when we comfort the suffering and confront the accusing. We like to imagine that we won't suffer as others do because we avoid evil. If Job can be blamed, then the equation of justice adds up. Job's friends fault him for encouraging others amid suffering but struggling to cope under his own strain (Job 4:4–5). Back and forth the friends debate, all the way to Job 38.

Then God speaks—from a whirlwind, in case we forget this is God talking now. The God who sanctioned this suffering now issues a challenge to Job, his righteous example.

> Who is this that darkens counsel by words without
>   knowledge?
> Dress for action like a man;
>   I will question you, and you make it known to me.
>
> Where were you when I laid the foundation of the
>   earth?
>   Tell me, if you have understanding.
> Who determined its measurements—surely you
>   know!
>   Or who stretched the line upon it?
> On what were its bases sunk,
>   or who laid its cornerstone,
> when the morning stars sang together
>   and all the sons of God shouted for joy?
>   (Job 38:2–7)

In the world God created, even the stars can sing. They were made to reflect the majesty of God in worship. "Shall a faultfinder contend with the Almighty?" God asks Job.

"He who argues with God, let him answer it" (Job 40:2). We sympathize with Job, cowering under this torrent of words. Compared with Job, we are far less holy, far less notable for our righteousness. Yet we too have grumbled against God. Job tries to still the whirlwind. He promises silence.

> Behold, I am of small account; what shall
>   I answer you?
>   I lay my hand on my mouth.
> I have spoken once, and I will not answer;
>   twice, but I will proceed no further. (Job 40:4–5)

Job offers to appease God with his silence. But God continues his rebuke until, mercifully, Job repents—back in the ashes (Job 42:6). Before this, he has only heard the voice of God. But now, in God's vivid depiction of the great sea creature Leviathan, Job sees the Creator in his rightful splendor. He says,

> Hear, and I will speak;
>   I will question you, and you make it known
>   to me. (Job 42:4)

If we're paying close attention, this exchange may surprise us. God is not asking for silence. When we suffer and do not understand, he is not demanding the stiff upper lip. He does not object to our groanings, our pleas for help, our desperate whimpers when we can't even form words. He does not need us to piece ourselves together before we say our *Thee*'s and *Thou*'s in formal prayer. He invites us to question him.

God is not threatened by our questions. Neither should we, then, tell the suffering to silence their complaints. But they must take their accusations straight to God—and listen.

Intercession Needed

Everywhere you look in the Hebrew Bible, you'll see exchanges between God and the patriarchs, prophets, or kings. God does not shrink before our speech. Wiesel's *Night* has thousands of years of pedigree. If anything, as we see amid the calamity of invasion at the outset of the prophet Isaiah's ministry, God invites this dialogue.

> Come now, let us reason together, says the Lord:
> though your sins are like scarlet,

> they shall be as white as snow;
>
> though they are red like crimson,
>
> > they shall become like wool. (Isa. 1:18)

Throughout the Bible you'll see the need for intercession in these conversations. We ask God for help in our trouble, but he requires a mediator. For us today, this aspect of a relationship with God probably makes the least sense. His holiness rests lightly on us. We feel little to no weight when we're before him. It's more comfortable to imagine God needing to answer us than us needing to answer to God. We imagine God's silence as his problem, not ours. He's responsible to answer. We're the ones asking the questions. The suffering of innocent children and the magnitude of the Holocaust prove to many skeptics today that God is silent because he doesn't exist, or because he's malevolent.

As we've already seen, however, the Scriptures and human experience reveal the problems with that assumption. We can't judge others without inviting judgment ourselves. We don't just need evil to be eradicated *out there*. We need it removed *in here*, within us. We're not as bad as Hitler. But that doesn't make us good.

As Job feels tormented by the harsh words of his friends, he expects vindication from God. His flesh may fail, but one day he will see God; he will one day be delivered from his calamity, his captivity in this world of sin. Yes, Job will be redeemed.

> For I know that my Redeemer lives,
>   and at the last he will stand upon the earth.
>   (Job 19:25)

In Job, we see a multilayered answer to our complaints about God's silence in the face of inexplicable suffering. To Elie Wiesel, Ivan Karamazov, and all others overwhelmed by the sin of this world, God invites dialogue. He accepts our lament. He asks us to reason with him. After all, we're made in his image. But we don't reason on equal terms. He is God. We are not. To approach him in his holiness, we need a mediator, because those who suffer still sin. We do not merely need deliverance from the evil of the world. We need deliverance from the evil in our hearts.

God's response to Job reveals another aspect of his relationship to us. Even to Job, the fullness of God remains obscured. God tames Leviathan without trouble, but he's hidden from us. He invites our speech, but sometimes he remains silent. Job errs in accusing his Creator because God's purposes often transcend our comprehension (Job 42:3). When we offer comfort, it's not usually wise to offer specific reasons for the suffering. And when challenging the skeptic, we often lack insight for why God allows particular evil.

Even the prophets often failed to comprehend God's plans. Consider how the prophets speak of Israel's exile from the promised land.

Like Job, the prophet Habakkuk opens with a complaint against God for his people's suffering. How could God be silent in the face of such injustice?

> O LORD, how long shall I cry for help,
>   and you will not hear?
> Or cry to you "Violence!"
>   and you will not save? (Hab. 1:2)

God's answer reminds us of his exchange with Job. God's purposes sometimes remain obscure even when we're looking to understand, even when we hear the reasons.

> Look among the nations, and see;
> > wonder and be astounded.
> For I am doing a work in your days
> > that you would not believe if told. (Hab. 1:5)

Habakkuk can't understand how God could use the evil of the Chaldeans to accomplish his good plan. In Habakkuk, as in Job, we see that God is not silent before evil. That's because he speaks through a prophet made in his image as he demands justice. These words, after all, have been preserved for us in the Scriptures. Moreover, God responds that he's doing something as Creator that we can't understand.

Once again we see how Wiesel's cries in the night follow a long-standing Jewish pattern before God. Psalm 88 might be considered the paradigm. The psalmist opens with an appeal to God:

> O Lord, God of my salvation,
> > I cry out day and night before you.
> Let my prayer come before you;
> > incline your ear to my cry! (vv. 1–2)

He senses that God has gone silent.

> But I, O Lord, cry to you;
> in the morning my prayer comes before you.
> O Lord, why do you cast my soul away?
> Why do you hide your face from me? (vv. 13–14)

Unlike so many other Hebrew prayers, including those of Habakkuk and Job, Psalm 88 ends without resolution. It ends, in fact, with night. It's like Wiesel's memoir and Job cursing the day he was born.

> You have caused my beloved and my friend to
> shun me;
> my companions have become darkness. (v. 18)

For anyone who has suffered depression, God's word here offers comfort. Even the psalmist felt like darkness was his only friend. We are not alone—even when we cannot seem to hear God. This short booklet can hardly contain all the examples in Scripture, especially in the Psalms, of people crying out to God and hearing nothing in response. Here's King David:

> My God, my God, why have you forsaken me?
>> Why are you so far from saving me, from the
>> words of my groaning?
> O my God, I cry by day, but you do not answer,
>> and by night, but I find no rest. (Ps. 22:1–2)

Now here's where Scripture really takes a turn. The next time we hear this prayer, it's from a man whose companions have shunned him. His friends have fled. The world has become shrouded in darkness. From parched lips we hear a loud voice cry out, "Eloi, Eloi, lema sabachthani?" He's quoting Psalm 22:1: "My God, my God, why have you forsaken me?"

It's the prayerful plea of Jesus as he hangs dying on the cross (Mark 15:34). It's the final cry of a Son for his Father.

Some bystanders speculate that Jesus is calling for Elijah. Perhaps the great Hebrew prophet will arrive with a thunderclap and rescue Jesus from his agony. After all, Malachi foretold that God would send Elijah before the "great and awesome day of the Lord" (Mal. 4:5). The crowd watches and waits. They look to the heavens. If the Father recognizes Jesus as his Son, surely he will rescue him. Do not Jesus's own disciples—indeed, his own mother and brothers and friends—expect deliverance?

Jesus told them Elijah would come to "restore all things" (Mark 9:12). Together on the mountain, Peter, James, and John have seen Jesus with Elijah and Moses. They've heard the Father speak from a cloud, "This is my beloved Son; listen to him" (Mark 9:7). They've heard a similar message when Jesus was baptized by his cousin John, whom Matthew named as the Elijah to come (Matt. 11:14). As Jesus emerged from the Jordan River, a voice from heaven said, "This is my beloved Son, with whom I am well pleased" (Matt. 3:16–17).

Surely, then, this is the moment for truth to prevail. As the Father has spoken blessing on the Son twice earlier, in the presence of Elijah and his successor, surely he will deliver now before it's too late.

The Son gives one last agonized cry. One last labored breath.

From the Father we hear nothing. Only silence.

Night has never been darker. Quiet has never been quieter.

How could this man claim to be the Son of God?

Suffering Servant

Was Jesus mistaken? Were his disciples? For Jesus, this silence meant violence. Hanging on the Romans' most notorious method of murder, he received no reprieve from his agony.

How should we understand what was happening? How does this experience speak to those who suffer not only physical pain but also the absence of God? For a clue, we need to head back to the great Jewish prophet Isaiah. In Isaiah 53:7–9, he spoke this word from God about a suffering servant:

> He was oppressed, and he was afflicted,
>   yet he opened not his mouth;
> like a lamb that is led to the slaughter,
>   and like a sheep that before its shearers is silent,
>   so he opened not his mouth.
> By oppression and judgment he was taken away;
>   and as for his generation, who considered
> that he was cut off out of the land of the living,
>   stricken for the transgression of my people?
> And they made his grave with the wicked

and with a rich man in his death,
although he had done no violence,
and there was no deceit in his mouth.

The lamb led to the slaughter. He opened not his mouth. Think back to Jesus before Dostoevsky's Grand Inquisitor. He offered no defense but a kiss. *Only silence.*

Whatever others may have thought about the Father's silence, Jesus wasn't surprised. He taught his disciples to expect nothing less. The Son must go to Jerusalem and suffer many things before dying at the hands of the elders and chief priests and scribes (Matt. 16:21). Such is the fate of prophets who speak the truth in a world that fell with a lie. John had come as Elijah, and his head ended up on a platter (Matt. 14:1–12). Jesus knew the history. He cried, "O Jerusalem, Jerusalem, the city that kills the prophets and stones those who are sent to it!" (Matt. 23:37).

Other prophets had died *because of* the hard hearts of the people. But this prophet would be different. This prophet died *for* the hard hearts of the people. Like righteous Job, Jesus interceded with a sacrifice for his loved ones (Job 1:5). As Isaiah had foretold, an innocent servant's suffering would pardon his people's transgression.

His chastisement brings peace. By his wounds, our world will be healed (Isa. 53:5).

Sounds of Salvation

The Father may have been silent as Jesus died on the cross. But that's not because the Son had been abandoned. Jesus told the disciples that he would lay down his life for his sheep (John 10:15–16). He explained how it was all in accordance with the Father's will.

> For this reason the Father loves me, because I lay down my life that I may take it up again. No one takes it from me, but I lay it down of my own accord. I have authority to lay it down, and I have authority to take it up again. This charge I have received from my Father. (John 10:17–18)

The sounds of salvation that emanated from the hill outside Jerusalem called Golgotha were the cries of the Son of God. For six hours, the Creator and Sustainer of the universe hung on a Roman cross, slowly dying. In solidarity with its Maker, the land descended into the darkness of night (Mark 15:33).

This Son offered friendship to all but made enemies of those who claimed to speak for God while they made every follower "twice as much a child of hell" (Matt. 23:15). The Son's every good deed, his every healing miracle, enraged the self-righteous. In their show trials, they couldn't find a single transgression by Jesus. Still, these religious and political leaders threatened by Jesus's innocence silenced his prophetic voice.

Then, on the third day, the sun rose. Light shone on Jerusalem. The women who loved Jesus went to his tomb. "An angel of the Lord descended from heaven." The sound was deafening. The earth shook while he rolled the stone away from the tomb. The light was blinding. "His appearance was like lightning, and his clothing white as snow" (Matt. 28:2–3). He came with news of a new creation.

The former things had passed way. "In Christ God was reconciling the world to himself" (2 Cor. 5:19). That serpent of lies? Jesus crushed his power on the cross (Gen. 3:15).

"For our sake he made him to be sin who knew no sin," we read in 2 Corinthians 5:21, "so that in him we might become the righteousness of God." Theologians call this the great exchange. In our union with Christ, he takes on our sin and dies the death we deserved on the cross. He gives us the righteousness of his sinless life so one day we'll hear from our Father, "Well done, good and faithful servant" (Matt. 25:23).

God Has a Son

For now, at least a little while longer, the sounds of slaughter still haunt every corner of the earth. "Never again" gives way to terrorists on paragliders attacking youth during a music festival. Another land war in Europe yields war crimes in familiar Ukrainian cities. The League of Nations couldn't stop the last major war. The United Nations can't stop wars today. Over the clanging gong of breaking news, we listen for the first notes from a trumpet that will signal the end of evil (Matt. 24:31). Then, final judgment will be rendered to the butchers of Buchenwald and Berdychiv. No evil word will go unpunished. On that day, every child's cries will find consolation.

For God himself has a Son. Though he did no wrong, that Son suffered. And his suffering availed to our eternal salvation. This sheep may have been silent. But his sacrifice silenced the original accuser. The first enemy can rage. In the end, however, Satan cannot win.

Even now, God prepares to send his Son again. In Christ, new creation is coming. Jesus overcomes evil with good (see Rom. 12:21). He's making all things new (Rev. 21:5).

When Christ returns, all who believe will kiss the lips that were betrayed. Jesus will wipe away every tear from our eyes. Death will be no more!

No mourning. No crying. No pain. We'll hear

a great multitude, like the roar of many waters and like the sound of mighty peals of thunder, crying out,

"Hallelujah!
For the Lord our God
the Almighty reigns." (Rev. 19:6)

God is never silent. His sheep hear his voice (John 10:27). Through the noise of this evil age, God's beloved hear the most reassuring promise of all: "I give them eternal life, and they will never perish, and no one will snatch them out of my hand" (John 10:28).

He hears your cries. He sees your tears.

Your Father may not give you an explanation. He gives you more—his Son (John 3:16).

When You Are Helping Someone Who Has Suffered

Job points the way for those of us who want to help our loved ones who suffer from God's silence. Raise your voice to God on their behalf! Weep with them. Lament the evil of our fallen world. Get down in the dust to comfort them. And with full dignity as God's image bearers, speak up against the evil and injustice they've suffered (Job 2:12–13).

Job's friends started well, at least before they began to speak. Even when you need to speak, it's wise to start by listening, probably for longer than you expect. If someone wants you to teach, they'll likely insist on it. Your consistent, physical presence is more of a gift than you probably realize.

Job's friends went wrong when they demanded a formula that would explain Job's suffering. That way, they could understand why he deserved his fate and they didn't. They would have been better to stay quiet. If you don't know what to say to your suffering friend, read Scripture out loud. You and your loved one may be surprised by how raw the prayers of Scripture sound compared with the sanitized church voices many use today.

WHERE IS GOD IN A WORLD WITH SO MUCH EVIL?

Among common objections to God, this problem of evil probably tops the list. Whether you're talking with someone who suffers or debating someone who raises this question as an academic exercise, acknowledge that God does not usually give us specific reasons why he allows evil. His purposes often remain a mystery. It's not wise, for example, to offer arguments for why God allowed the Holocaust. He has not revealed those reasons to us.

However, you can gently inquire whether any alternatives satisfy our sense of justice. Does it help to imagine that God is not powerful enough to stop evil? Or that he hears our prayers and cannot do anything about them? Or that we live in a dark, cold universe where nothing matters except the will of the strong to abuse the weak? Or that if everyone would just agree not to be Hitler, we'd live together in peace?

Instead, isn't it more likely that we derive our sense of outrage at injustice from being made in the image of God? That if God does exist, his reasons might sometimes surpass our understanding? And that God sent his blameless Son to solve the problem of evil inside all our hearts? Consider: How else can we help the oppressed shun the temptation to turn their suffering into oppression of others?

When You Are Suffering Yourself

If you have believed Jesus is the Son of God and followed him with passion, the silence of God can be disorienting. C. S. Lewis said that God shouts in our pain, but that's not how everyone suffers.[13] Like Job's friends, we may wonder if we suffer because we've done something wrong. Or maybe we go so far as to question whether God has been merely a figment of our imagination.

As we've seen throughout the Bible, the Father wants us to cry out to him. He invites dialogue that emerges from trust in him. He expects lament. He may not answer the question you're asking. But if you believe in the Son, then God intends only good for you (Rom. 8:28). While our enemies may intend evil, God only works good (Gen. 50:20). He always has a purpose, though it may be hidden on this side of eternity.

When you can't hear God, look to the cross and you'll find him. There we receive assurance that justice will be done against all evil (Rom. 3:26). Any unrepentant Nazis who beat Elie Wiesel's father to death will pay the ultimate penalty in eternity. No evil escapes God's justice. But that's also a warning to us, because "all have sinned and fall short of the glory of God" (Rom. 3:23). We're not justified because Hitler is a worse sinner. We're justified when, like Job, we repent of our sins, big and small.

When I suffer, God's voice in Habakkuk 3:17–19 ministers to me.

> Though the fig tree should not blossom,
>   nor fruit be on the vines,
> the produce of the olive fail
>   and the fields yield no food,
> the flock be cut off from the fold
>   and there be no herd in the stalls,
> yet I will rejoice in the LORD;
>   I will take joy in the God of my salvation.
> GOD, the Lord, is my strength;
>   he makes my feet like the deer's;
>   he makes me tread on my high places.

It was a fig tree that Jesus cursed on his way to Jerusalem, where he would climb Calvary's hill (Mark 11:14). Jesus explained the lesson to his disciples in Mark 11:24:

"Therefore I tell you, whatever you ask in prayer, believe that you have received it, and it will be yours." That's the encouragement of Habakkuk. Though God may be silent, keep talking to him. Eventually your talking will turn into rejoicing in the Lord. Eventually your rejoicing will turn into dancing in his strength.

Evil doesn't have the last word in eternity. Jesus will make sure of that. In the meantime, he tells us how to manage. We forgive. And when we forgive, we remember our own trespasses the Father has forgiven (Mark 11:25).

Nothing was more antithetical to Hitler's agenda than forgiveness. He stoked grievance. He pursued enemies. Decades since most of them have died, the Nazis would be happy to learn they killed God, especially a Jew who preached that the meek will inherit the earth, that peacemakers will be called God's sons (Matt. 5:5, 9).

And yet, Jesus lives. And he speaks. When we protest injustice, when we forgive rather than avenge, when we comfort the children as they cry.

Notes

1. Elie Wiesel, *Night* (New York: Hill and Wang, 1958), 34.
2. Wiesel, *Night*, 64.
3. Wiesel, *Night*, 65.
4. Alec Ryrie, *Unbelievers: An Emotional History of Doubt* (Cambridge, MA: Belknap, 2019), 202.
5. Ryrie, *Unbelievers*, 203.
6. Ryrie, *Unbelievers*, 203.
7. I owe much of what I know about Dostoevsky and the problem of evil to my Northwestern University professor Gary Saul Morson. You can learn his perspective in the book *Wonder Confronts Certainty: Russian Writers on the Timeless Questions and Why Their Answers Matter* (Cambridge, MA: Belknap, 2023).

8. Fyodor Dostoevsky, *The Brothers Karamazov*, bicentennial ed., trans. Richard Pevear and Larissa Volokhonsky (New York: Picador, 1990), 260–61.
9. Dostoevsky, *The Brothers Karamazov*, 261.
10. Dostoevsky, *The Brothers Karamazov*, 279.
11. Vasily Grossman, *Life and Fate*, trans. Robert Chandler (New York: Harper & Row, 1985), 554.
12. Aleksandr Solzhenitsyn, *The Gulag Archipelago, 1918–1956: An Experiment in Literary Investigation*, vol. 2, pts. 3–4, trans. Thomas P. Whitney (New York: Harper & Row, 1975), 615.
13. C. S. Lewis, *The Problem of Pain* (1940; repr., New York: HarperCollins, 1996), 91.

Recommended Resources

Carson, D. A. *How Long, O Lord? Reflections on Suffering and Evil.* Grand Rapids, MI: Baker, 2006. Don't pass along this book unless you know someone wants to dig deeper into the biblical and theological accounts about evil and suffering. This is the best overview of the subject, but it is probably not the place to start when a person's suffering remains raw.

Douglass, Frederick. *Narrative of the Life of Frederick Douglass, an American Slave.* Boston: Anti-Slavery Office, 1845. The African American church shares with the Jewish tradition a rich history of lament. Douglass captures the nature of evil in his descriptions of his supposedly Christian owners. But his life also testifies to the power of a voice raised in God's name against injustice.

Keller, Timothy. *Hope in Times of Fear: The Resurrection and the Meaning of Easter*. New York: Viking, 2021. If the resurrection is true, then everything changes for our suffering. And if you don't already believe that the resurrection really happened, this book will make you want it to be true.

Keller, Timothy. *Walking with God through Pain and Suffering*. New York: Penguin, 2015. Keller doesn't just walk through the scriptural witness about suffering; he also introduces you to the testimonies of friends throughout the Bible and history who have heard God's words of comfort in their affliction.

Ten Boom, Corrie. *The Hiding Place*. Grand Rapids, MI: Chosen, 1971. Like Elie Wiesel, Corrie ten Boom suffered in a Nazi concentration camp. Like Wiesel, she also lost a sister to the Nazis. But this book offers a compelling Christian contrast to Wiesel's skepticism.

Vroegop, Mark. *Dark Clouds, Deep Mercy: Discovering the Grace of Lament*. Wheaton, IL: Crossway, 2019. This is an especially good place to start to help someone who is suffering to develop the language of biblical lament, especially if your Christian tradition doesn't usually pray that way.

Scripture Index

Genesis
1:1–3 18
1:26 19
3:8 20
3:9 20
3:15 37
3:17 20
50:20 42

Job
book of 20, 30
1:1 21
1:5 35
1:21 21
2:8 21
2:9 21
2:10 21
2:12 22
2:12–13 40
3:3–10 23
4:4–5 23

4:7 23
19:25 28
38 23
38:2–7 24
40:2 25
40:4–5 25
42:3 29
42:4 25
42:6 25

Psalms
book of 31
22:1 32
22:1–2 32
88 .... 30, 31
88:1–2 30
88:13–14 31
88:18 31

Isaiah
1:18 27
53:5 36
53:7–9 34

SCRIPTURE INDEX

Habakkuk
book of 30
1:2 29
1:5 30
3:17–19 43

Malachi
4:5 32

Matthew
3:16–17 33
5:5 44
5:9 44
11:14 33
14:1–12 35
16:21 35
23:15 37
23:37 35
24:31 38
25:23 38
28:2–3 37

Mark
9:7 33
9:12 33
11:14 43

11:24 43
11:25 44
15:33 36
15:34 32

John
3:16 39
10:15–16 36
10:17–18 36
10:27 39
10:28 39

Romans
3:23 43
3:26 42
8:28 42
12:21 39

2 Corinthians
5:19 37
5:21 37

Revelation
19:6 39
21:5 39

TGC | THE GOSPEL COALITION

The Gospel Coalition (TGC) supports the church in making disciples of all nations, by providing gospel-centered resources that are trusted and timely, winsome and wise.

Guided by a Council of more than 40 pastors in the Reformed tradition, TGC seeks to advance gospel-centered ministry for the next generation by producing content (including articles, podcasts, videos, courses, and books) and convening leaders (including conferences, virtual events, training, and regional chapters).

In all of this we want to help Christians around the world better grasp the gospel of Jesus Christ and apply it to all of life in the 21st century. We want to offer biblical truth in an era of great confusion. We want to offer gospel-centered hope for the searching.

Join us by visiting TGC.org so you can be equipped to love God with all your heart, soul, mind, and strength, and to love your neighbor as yourself.

TGC.org

TGC HARD QUESTIONS

Does God Care about Gender Identity?
Samuel D. Ferguson

Is Christianity Good for the World?
Sharon James

What Does Depression Mean for My Faith?
Kathryn Butler, MD

Why Do We Feel Lonely at Church?
Jeremy Linneman

Where Is God in a World with So Much Evil?
Colin Hansen

Did the Resurrection Really Happen?
Timothy Paul Jones

The series TGC Hard Questions serves the church by providing tools that answer people's deep *longings* for community, their *concerns* about biblical ethics, and their *doubts* about confessional faith.

For more information, visit **crossway.org**.